Cuida tus modales / Minding Our Manners

No acoses / Don't Be a Bully

Frances Nagle
Traducido por Eida de la Vega

Gareth Stevens PUBLISHING

conceptos básicos

Un acosador es alguien que trata de lastimar o hacer sentir mal a otra persona.

A bully is someone who tries to hurt another person or make them feel bad.

DECISION POINT
COST-BENEFIT ANALYSIS for EXECUTIVE DECISION MAKING
Smart Questions
EFFECTIVE MEETINGS FOR BUSY PEOPLE

Algunos acosadores lastiman a otros golpeándolos o empujándolos.

Some bullies hurt others by hitting or pushing them.

Otros acosadores dicen
cosas crueles.

Other bullies
say mean things.

Hay muchas razones por las que los acosadores lastiman a otros. Quizás piensan que así van a ser aceptados.

There are many reasons why bullies hurt people. They might want to fit in.

Los acosadores piensan que son importantes si hacen sentir mal a otros.

Bullies try to feel important by making others feel bad.

Los acosadores con frecuencia se meten con personas que son diferentes.

Bullies often pick on people who are different.

Es posible que el acosador no sepa cómo enfrentar los problemas de una manera sana.

A bully might not know how to deal with problems in a healthy way.

Uno se puede sentir enojado o dolido, pero no hay razón para acosar a nadie.

It is okay to feel angry or hurt. But there is no good reason to bully someone.

Tómate un tiempo para calmarte. Después discute cualquier problema que tengas.

Take time to calm down. Then, talk about any problems you have.

Piensa en cómo te sentirías si te acosaran.

Think about how you would feel if you were being bullied.

Defiende a los que son acosados. ¡Te sentirás bien ayudando a los demás!

Stand up for those who are being bullied. You will feel good helping others!

5
+ 3
7
+ 4
6
4
+ 3
Love

Please visit our website, www.garethstevens.com. For a free color catalog of all our high-quality books, call toll free 1-800-542-2595 or fax 1-877-542-2596.

Library of Congress Cataloging-in-Publication Data

Nagle, Frances.
Don't be a bully = No acoses / by Frances Nagle.
p. cm. — (Minding Our Manners = Cuida tus modales)
Parallel title: Cuida tus modales.
In English and Spanish.
Includes index.
ISBN 978-1-4824-1623-7 (library binding)
1. Bullying — Juvenile literature. I. Title.
BF637.B85 N34 2015
302.3—d23

First Edition

Published in 2015 by
Gareth Stevens Publishing
111 East 14th Street, Suite 349
New York, NY 10003

Designer: Andrea Davison-Bartolotta
Editor: Kristen Rajczak
Spanish Translation: Eida de la Vega

Photo credits: Cover, p. 1 (main) stefanolunardi/Shutterstock.com; cover, back cover, p. 1 (blue background) Eky Studio/Shutterstock.com; p. 3 Fuse/Thinkstock; p. 5 Twin Design/Shutterstock.com; p. 7 LWA/The Image Bank/Getty Images; p. 9 BananaStock/Thinkstock; p. 11 Craig Dingle/E+/Getty Images; p. 13 Stephen Coburn/Shutterstock.com; p. 15 Cultra RM/Anni Engel/Collection Mix: Subjects/Getty Images; p. 17 JillianSuzanne/iStock/Thinkstock; p. 19 Jupiterimages/Pixland/Thinkstock; p. 21 Jupiterimages/Creatas/Thinkstock; p. 23 iofoto/Shutterstock.com.

Printed in the United States of America

CPSIA compliance information: Batch #CW15GS: For further information contact Gareth Stevens, New York, New York at 1-800-542-2595.